Second Edition

Camp Is for the Camper

A Counselor's Guide to Youth Development

An American Camp Association Book

Connie Coutellier

enriching lives, building tomorrows

Disclaimer

This book provides an overview of issues with which camp counselors should be familiar. It should be recognized that camp staff who lead campers may require further education and experience in each of the areas covered herein. Neither the publisher nor the author of this book undertake to verify that individuals who use this book are trained appropriately. Nor do the publisher or author assume any responsibility for liability for any consequences of the use of information in this book. Further, the American Camp Association, Inc. and the author hereby expressly disclaim any responsibility, liability, or duty to camp administrators, operators, personnel, any program participants, or their families, for any such liability arising out of injury, illness, or loss to any person or organization.

ISBN: 978-1-58518-041-7
Library of Congress Control Number: 2007922622
Cover design: Bean Creek Studio
Book layout: Bean Creek Studio
Front and back cover photos and text photos: Suz Welch, Boone, Iowa; Camp Hantesa, Heart of the Hawkeye Council of Camp Fire USA, Boone, Iowa

Healthy Learning
P.O. Box 1828
Monterey, CA 93942
www.healthylearning.com

American Camp Association
5000 State Rd. 67 North
Martinsville, IN 46151
www.acacamps.org

Contents

The Camp Environment

Responsibility as a Role Model

Camp as a Positive Force in Youth Development

First Sight/Arrival

The First Day/Night

Stress 24/7

Child Abuse

Social Trends

Parent Interaction or Interference

Developmental Characteristics

Age Characteristics Chart

Reinforcing Positive Behaviors

Courtesies of Group Living

Understanding Behavior Clues

Missing Home (Homesickness)

Bed-wetting

ADD/ADHD

Aggression and Violence

Self-Mutilating Behaviors (SMB)

Suicide

Eating Disorders

AIDS

Dealing with inappropriate Behaviors

Camper Behavior Management Guide

About This Book

Camp Is for the Camper is designed to help you discuss preventions and interventions with your director and other counselors and to teach you the following:

- your responsibilities as a role model
- tips to survive the stress of your first experiences supervising a camper group
- the characteristics and program considerations for your camper-age group
- suggestions for reinforcing positive behaviors and for dealing with inappropriate behaviors of individual campers and camper groups

The primary purpose of this book is to provide a resource to help assist camp counselors in working more effectively with their campers. The author has gathered information through discussions with camp directors, workshops, and years of her own practical experience as a camping professional. This book can serve as a discussion starter in counselor training. The camp will need to identify specific policies and procedures, as well as the appropriate and inappropriate behaviors pertaining to their camp and clientele. The author and the American Camp Association encourage both counselors and other camp personnel to seek additional information and training in this area. My appreciations and sincere thanks to Kathy Henchey for her contributions to the first edition of this book.

A Unique Opportunity

Camp. What a great job!...What fun!...What a rush! Spending your summer engaging in outdoor activities at camp with campers gives you a unique opportunity to contribute to the growth and development of the children in your care. You have been hired because your director believes you are capable of using good judgment, demonstrating teamwork, having concern for others, and making a positive contribution to campers and the camp community.

The Camp Environment

The camp community is unique. It is a community of persons living, working, and playing together as an organized, democratic group in an outdoor setting. Similar to society, the camp community usually takes shape in small groups, like family groups, except the campers in the small group are about the same age. These small groups are often a part of a larger unit or neighborhood. These neighborhoods of different age groups join to form an intentional youth-focused camp community. Staff, in a variety of roles, provide the trained leadership to make the community function effectively. What occurs in the camp community as the relationships between peers and adults develop is critical to the success of the experience. While camp is an informal and intense experience, it occurs in a relaxed, open atmosphere that provides adventure, fun, and relief from the daily pressures and stresses of the campers' home community.

Responsibility as a Role Model

Your status is also unique. You have neither the rights of a parent nor the responsibilities of a director, yet you exert tremendous influence on campers through your close contact with them. Your influence is extremely important because children tend to imitate their adult role models. The example you set reflects your own values, expectations, background, and experiences. Parents have entrusted their most precious possession to you—their child. They are allowing you to be a partner in the development of their child. Realizing that their child is looking up to you, they expect you to not only provide a safe and enjoyable experience, but to help their child develop the skills necessary to become caring, competent, successful adults.

Camp as a Positive Force in Youth Development

Each camp has specific goals and desired outcomes for its campers. Beyond providing a fun and safe outdoor experience for children, camps contribute to positive youth development. In this regard, they help children develop the skills needed to become productive and connected, and able to navigate in their relatively complex world. These competencies are best achieved when the camp provides opportunities for:

- meaningful relationships with positive role models
- exploration of self and the environment
- informal interaction with peers
- experiences that are inherently interesting and fun
- physical activity
- safe experiences, with limits and supervision
- structured reflection on the experience

Beyond providing a fun and safe outdoor experience for children, camps contribute to positive youth development.

Since the turn of the century, the American Camp Association has been conducting research on the youth development outcomes of the camp experience and ways to continuously improve the experience for more children. For additional information in this area, refer to research information on the ACA website at www.acacamps.org.

It is important that you understand your camp's purpose, goals, and desired outcomes for the campers in your care. Review the camp brochure and discuss what your camp has promised parents. Know what your role is in accomplishing these outcomes and how you are expected to contribute.

First Sight /Arrival

Don't panic! The most important time to establish a positive relationship with your campers and help them become comfortable is during your first meeting with them. Keep in mind that as you are checking out your camper group, they are sizing you up too. They are asking themselves, "Will this person care about me and be on my side, and are we going to play, work, and be friends?" You can do a number of things to help make campers feel at ease, including:

- Smile; be enthusiastic and cheerful.
- Look them in the eye and say their name.
- Make them feel that they are important by letting them know you are happy they are at camp.
- Help them say good-bye to their parents and join their camper group.
- Start a conversation with them; find out what makes them unique, what they like, and what they want to do at camp.
- Try to get to know each camper and help them get to know the other members of their group.

The First Day/Night

The first-day events set the tone for the rest of the campers' stay at camp. Be sure that campers know how their needs will be met. When all campers arrive, have several age-appropriate, get-acquainted games ready to play. Plan activities that have the group work as a team. Schedule a tour of camp, and when campers are feeling comfortable with their surroundings and each other, it is time to discuss the schedule for their next day(s) at camp. Discuss what they will be doing and when. Talk to them about the rules that they will need to follow so that everyone will have fun and a safe experience at camp.

If you are working at a resident camp, preparing for bedtime on the first night is difficult for everyone. You have probably just gotten back from break and tried to cram everything you needed to do in a 24-hour period. New campers have arrived and are worried, scared, or worst—missing home (homesick). At this point, you will need all the patience you have and more. Plan an evening activity that starts out very active and finishes up with a quiet activity, such as reading or telling stories, nothing scary. This is a good time to talk about what night noises they might hear and what those noises are. When you have reassured the group and answered all their questions and concerns, it's time for bed. Spend some time with each camper to determine whether you have calmed fears and made him or her comfortable for the night.

Stress 24/7

To say camp is an intense experience is probably like saying you can't have s'mores without marshmallows. Camp possesses you and the camper completely; you are at camp with almost no outside influences or distractions. A camp counselor may spend as much or more time with campers than the campers' parents are able to spend—particularly in the resident-camp situation, where staff members are often with campers 24 hours a day, day after day. Even with time off, a counselor can find him or herself burnt out by the end of the fourth or fifth week of camp. Time off may actually cause additional stress when you're pressured to be with friends, do laundry, drive distances, etc. Living in close quarters with others, while performing demanding and physically challenging duties, can lead to a decrease in your level of tolerance. When you are exhausted or getting angry at campers and other staff, you can take the following steps to reduce stress and enjoy the summer:

- Make sure you get enough sleep.
- Maintain a good sense of humor.
- Eat well.
- Make time for yourself.
- Recognize your limits.
- Find someone in whom you can confide. Resolve problems quickly.
- Be patient with other staff members, campers, and yourself.

A camp counselor may spend as much or more time with campers than the campers' parents are able to spend—particularly in the resident-camp situation, where staff members are often with campers 24 hours a day, day after day.

Child Abuse

Camp is a place where campers find adults they can trust and admire. Your campers may confide abusive behavior (i.e., physical, sexual, and/or emotional) that has occurred in the home environment or abusive behaviors by other staff or campers. Certain signs of emotional abuse (withdrawal, lack of self-esteem or self worth, constant need for approval, etc.) or sexual abuse (inappropriate sex play, unusual knowledge of sex for the child's age, etc.) should not be dismissed as normal human growth and development. Other symptoms identified by the National Center for Missing or Exploited Children include:

- Changes in behavior, extreme mood swings, withdrawal, fearfulness, and excessive crying
- Bed-wetting, nightmares, fear of going to bed, or wearing lots of clothes to bed
- Acting out inappropriate sexual activity or showing unusual interest in sexual matters
- Regression to infantile behavior
- A sudden acting out of feelings or aggressive or rebellious behavior
- A fear of certain places, people, or activities, especially of being alone with certain people
- Pain, itching, bleeding, fluid, or rawness in the private areas

Camp may also be a place where adults can build trusting relationships with campers. Your director should explain any policies regarding appropriate and inappropriate touching in camp, and how to handle any suspicion of abuse before, during, or after camp. In this regard, examples of general guidelines for counselor behavior when you're with campers include:

- Never touch a child against the child's will (verbally or nonverbally expressed), unless it is to prevent an accident.
- When others are present, it is usually okay to touch a child on the shoulders, arm, or upper back.
- Excessively tickling, wrestling with, or teasing a camper is inappropriate.
- "Hazing" or "initiations" by campers or staff that are abusive in any manner are unacceptable.
- It is inappropriate to share information about your personal sexuality or sex life.
- Don't show favoritism or encourage crushes or romantic fantasies that campers may have about you.
- Respect the privacy of campers during the times when they are changing clothes or showering.

- Young campers should be encouraged to change their own clothes.
- It is not appropriate to share a bed or sleeping bag with a camper.
- Never put yourself in a position where you are alone with a camper and not within sight of another staff member.
- Groups should have double coverage by staff or at least be within sight or sound of another staff member.
- Don't show signs of affection to other staff in front of campers. Remember: Camp is for the camper.

Directors carefully screen staff by securing references and background checks. However, if a child confides in you about another camper or staff member, discuss the disclosure personally with the director and refrain from investigating or discussing it with other staff. In most states, a camp's staff are "mandated reporters" and have a legal obligation to report child abuse to the authorities. The increase in camper-to-camper abuse is discussed in the section on group behavior. What may have been considered a prank or hazing in the past is often considered abuse today.

2

Today's Campers

Today, more than ever, day camps, resident camps, and other outdoor education and experiential activities have the potential to be a partner with parents in the growth and development of children. Yes, parents are looking for opportunities for fun and safe experiences for their children, but they are looking for more than that. To be fun and safe, children also need an emotionally safe environment where they can have "real-life" experiences, based on a knowledge of positive youth development. To realize this potential, camp staff must become more aware of the social and emotional needs of both children and parents. Campers are engaged in the undertaking of growing up. They are developing competencies, trying on new roles, learning social skills, and trying to control their feelings and impulses.

Social Trends

Technological advances, family dynamics, and changing populations impact camps and the children they serve. To better understand the behavior and background of your campers, you should be aware of the following social trends:

- Communication expectations of parents have changed with available technology. Campers often receive letters via fax and e-mail. In 2003, over 77 percent of all children ages 7-17 had access to a computer at home, up from 36 percent in 1994; 68 percent had access to the internet compared with 15 percent in 1994. Common uses for the home computer by children and youth include educational programs, games, word processing, and access to the Internet. (Techpolicybank)

- Both the proportion of children living in extreme poverty and those living in families with high income continues to increase, causing a growing income disparity among families with children and a decrease in the number of middle class families. (ChildStats)

- Beyond academic and social pressures, today's high school students also are concerned about their health. When asked to identify the biggest health problem facing young people today, obesity (24 percent), cigarette smoking (23 percent), and depression (21 percent) share the top spot on the list. (Horatio Alger Association—State of Our Nation's Youth 2005-2006)

- Students find open ears and good listeners at home. Fully nine in ten (90 percent) high school students say that they can confide in and talk to at least one family member about things. Not only has this finding been consistent over the past few years, it also is consistent across ethnic, geographic, and socioeconomic lines. (Horatio Alger Association—State of Our Nation's Youth 2005-2006)

- Even more than their parents, students depend on the internet to stay in touch with their friends, family, and the world. Fully 95 percent have access to the internet. In addition to the internet, more than three in five (62 percent) high school students have a cell phone. (Horatio Alger Association—State of Our Nation's Youth 2005-2006)

- The increasing percentage of overweight children is a public health challenge. In 1976-1980, only six percent of children ages 6-17 were overweight. By 1988-1994, this proportion had risen to 11 percent, and in 2003-2004, this proportion was 18 percent. (Child Stats) By the time an obese child is 13 or 14, his or her self-esteem is already significantly less than half that of normal-weight children. (*Pediatrics*)

- Forty percent of girls ages 11-17 say they do not play sports because they do not feel skilled or competent and 23 percent do not think their bodies look good. (*The New Normal: What Girls Say About Healthy Living GSRI, 2006*)

- Despite hitting the lowest level in 30 years, teen pregnancy rates are still high. In fact, 31 percent of teenage girls get pregnant at least once before they reach age 20. (The Guttmacher Institute, 2006)

- About 28 percent of families are headed by a single parent. (U.S. Census) Among children living with their mothers, nearly three quarters of the mothers work. Twenty-one percent of children 0-17 are living with at least one foreign-born parent. (Child Stats) Before they are eighteen years of age, almost half of the children born today will have parents who divorce.

- Studies show that between 15 to 25 percent of U.S. students are bullied with some frequency, while 15 to 20 percent report that they bully others with some frequency. Boys are more likely than girls to bully others. Girls frequently report being bullied by both boys and girls, but boys are most often bullied only by other boys. (USDHHS)

- In 2005, more than one out of ten (11 percent) high school females reported having been raped at some point in her life. One out of every 11 high school students was a victim of dating violence in 2005. (Child Trends)

- The percentage of teens who do not date at all has risen steadily since the early 1990s, reaching new highs in 2004. Among 10th graders, for example, rates rose from 28 percent in 1991 to 37 percent in 2004. (Child Trends)

- Between 1996 and 2005, daily cigarette use fell by more than half among both eighth grade students (from 10 percent to 4 percent, respectively) and tenth grade students (from 18 percent to 8 percent, respectively). Cigarette use has also been declining among twelfth graders, from 23 percent in 1999 to a new low of 14 percent in 2005. Youth who smoke are more likely to drink, to use other drugs, and to engage in a variety of other risky behaviors. They are also less likely to be physically fit and more likely to suffer from respiratory problems. (Child Trends)

- The percentage of children in the United States who are Hispanic more than doubled between 1980 and 2004, from 9 percent to 19 percent, and is projected to increase to nearly one-quarter (24 percent) of the child population by 2020. (Child Trends)

- From ages four to five, children stereotype gender behavior, express racial reasons for not playing with others, and show discomfort around people with disabilities. Between the ages of seven and nine, children develop what psychologists call "true racial attitudes," likely to be long lasting. (National Public Radio's Teacher Guide, "Prejudice Puzzle")

- Children spend nearly half of their discretionary time watching television. Black students are much more likely than white students to watch four or more hours of television per day on the average weekday. For example, among eighth graders in 2004, 57 percent of black students watched four or more hours of television, compared with 24 percent of white students. (Child Trends)

- Students who watched six or more hours of television each day scored lower, on average, than did other students on the National Assessment of Educational Progress (NAEP) mathematics assessment. In addition, excessive exposure to violent television programs may increase aggression levels. Recent research has shown that young adults who routinely watched violent television as children (6- to 10-year-olds) exhibit more aggressive behaviors as young adults than their peers who did not watch violent television. Research also finds that excessive television viewing at young ages (ages one to three) is linked with decreased attention span later on. (Child Trends)

- The percentage of children with asthma has increased over the past two decades, from 3 percent in 1981 to 6 percent in 2002, where it remained through 2004. Asthma is more common among boys than it is among girls. In 2004, 7 percent of males under age 18 had asthma, compared with 4 percent of females. (Child Trends) Nearly one in 13 school-aged children has asthma (National Center for Health Statistics). Six to eight percent of children with asthma have food allergies which can trigger asthma symptoms (Food Allergy Network). Several studies indicate that the prevalence of peanut allergy in children doubled over a recent five-year period.

So, what does this mean for the campers with whom you will be working? Take a few minutes to consider each of the aforementioned statements.

Parent Interaction or Interference

The aforementioned social trends describe common characteristics of families and children in the United States today. As our society grows more complex and lifestyles become more hectic, parents are struggling with deciding the right thing to do for their children. Most parents want a camp experience that will be fun and provide the kind of independent, healthy growth experience their child needs, but even more importantly, they want an experience that will be safe. For most children (and their parents), the transition from home to camp involves a period of adjustment that may even include some separation anxiety. The child must learn to function in a new setting without their parents.

As the time for camp arrives, the child may begin to feel anxious about leaving the comfort of a predictable environment. At this point, parents may also begin to question their decision about sending their child away to camp. They want to know more about the person who will be taking care of their child.

Most parents want a camp experience that will be fun and provide the kind of independent, healthy growth experience their child needs, but even more importantly, they want an experience that will be safe.

While you may feel that the adjustment to camp would be easier if there was less contact, parents, today, expect a different level of communication. Camps are trying to create a partnership with parents regarding the healthy development of their child. Be sure you understand your role in this partnership. Parents put their trust in you and have valuable information to share about their child. They don't expect you to be perfect. They do expect you to use good judgment, be attentive, and create an emotionally and physically safe environment for their child. If you have the opportunity to meet the parents or to talk with them during the session, it is important that you show real interest in their concerns and discuss ways to help their child have a successful camp experience. At the end of a camp session, don't be so anxious to begin your time off. Take a few minutes to talk to each parent and answer questions about their child's experience at camp.

Developmental Characteristics

Children are impressionable, flexible, easily led, understanding, occasionally cruel, more honest than they may ever again be, enthusiastic, at times frightened and insecure, eager for acceptance, success, adventure and fun, and have a strong need for understanding leadership. Children's behavior is not always consistent. One moment, a child can be charming and appealing, and, the next moment, seem to be a real "pain in the neck." Although not all children fit perfectly, the following chart will give you some ideas about the physical, social, emotional, and intellectual characteristics of the age groups with whom you will be working. The chart also includes several specific suggestions for activities and special considerations for each age group.

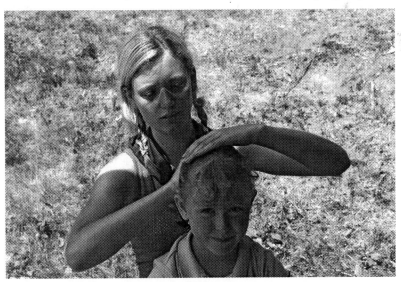

Children are impressionable, flexible, easily led, understanding, occasionally cruel, more honest than they may ever again be, enthusiastic, at times frightened and insecure, eager for acceptance, success, adventure and fun, and have a strong need for understanding leadership.

AGE CHARACTERISTICS CHART

FIVE-TO-SEVEN YEAR OLDS

Physical

- mastering physical skills (physical activities)
- exhibit better control of large muscles than small muscles
- engages in high-activity level (restless and fidgety)
- working on eye-hand coordination

Social

- learning to be friends and have "best" friends
- becoming more aware of peers and their opinions
- beginning to experience empathy for others
- are still family oriented (beginning to relate to non-family adults)
- becoming aware of sexual differences
- want to structure their environment as their home is structured
- want assurance of an adult's presence

Emotional

- see fairness as being nice to others so they will be nice in return
- seek parent and adult approval; behave in ways to avoid punishment
- developing modesty
- expressing feelings and emotions; upsets are usually short-term

Intellectual

- increasing attention span (activities best limited to 15 to 30 minutes)
- more interested in process than product
- learning to sort things into categories and arrange in a series
- learning concepts of right and wrong, cause and effect
- handle well only one mental operation at a time
- can distinguish between reality and fantasy, but may be afraid of scary figures

Activities and Special Considerations

Provide opportunities for:

- experimentation using bodies, ideas, and material in different ways
- active, boisterous games, climbing and balance, rhythmic activities
- practicing skills involving eye-hand coordination, such as cutting, pasting, drawing, etc.
- practice in group cooperation, sharing, and good work habits
- freedom to do things for themselves (no longer babies) and use and develop their own abilities
- using of senses requiring use of ears, eyes, nose, mouth, and skin
- reenacting routines and events of their known world
- developing friendship skills of sharing, helping, taking turns, and working with others
- finding appropriate ways of channeling emotions and behaviors

EIGHT-TO-TEN YEAR OLDS

Physical

- experience steady increases in large muscle development
- increased strength, balance, and coordination
- active with boundless energy, often restless and fidgety
- boys and girls maturing at differing rates (boys are slower to mature)
- increasing in manual dexterity, eye-hand, and small muscle coordination

Social

- see adults as authority
- follow rules out of respect for authority
- can be noisy and argumentative
- feel loyalty to friendship group, often with "secret" words identifies with same sex group
- expanded use of reasoning skills to solve problems, negotiate, and compromise

Emotional

- view right behavior as "obeying" rules set by those in power
- accept parent/family beliefs
- admire and imitate older boys and girls
- developing decision-making skills
- beginning to take responsibility for their own actions
- need acceptance from peer groups
- emphasize similarities between self and friends; look to adults for guidance and approval
- need involvement with caring adult
- comparisons with the success of others difficult and may erode of self-confidence
- self-conscious, afraid to fail, sensitive to criticism
- feel they can do no wrong and are quick to correct others
- name-calling and teasing are methods for responding to being upset
- feel too "cool" for emotions

Intellectual

- are quick, eager, and enthusiastic
- vary greatly in academic abilities, interests, and reasoning skills
- have an increased attention span, but interests change rapidly; beginning to think logically and symbolically
- learning to use good judgment
- beginning to learn about moral judgments, applying principles of right and wrong; want to know the how, what, and why of things
- see things as "black and white" and "yes and no" and have difficulty with opinions different than theirs

Eight-to-ten year olds have an increased attention span, but their interests change rapidly.

Activities and Special Considerations

Provide opportunities for:

- using large and small muscles in activities
- organizing team games and sports where everyone can be successful
- working in groups in cooperative activities
- using skills to explore and investigate the world
- assuming responsibility
- discussing other people's viewpoints
- exploring interests in collections and hobbies
- expressing feelings and imagination through creative writing or acting
- discussing reasonable explanations for rules and decisions
- are interested in making and doing "real" things and using "real" tools, equipment, and materials

ELEVEN-TO-THIRTEEN YEAR OLDS

Physical

- exhibit a wide range of sexual maturity and growth patterns between genders and within gender groups (girls are about two years ahead of boys)
- experience rapid change in physical appearance
- growth of hands and feet, nose, and ears may be faster than arms, legs, and face, causing concern for appearance
- may try experimental behavior to enhance sensory stimulation, e.g., drug and alcohol use

Social

- shifting from emphasis on same sex to opposite sex—girls develop interest in boys earlier than boys in girls
- looking more toward peers than parents; seeking peer recognition
- seeking acceptance and trust
- tend to regard sex in a depersonalized way
- searching for adult role models and often identifying with admired adult hairdos, dress, and mannerisms of popular sports and music stars

- question authority
- question family values
- willing to submerge self for benefit of group
- discipline can be a problem because of spirit of group
- friendship groups or cliques are often small but intense
- have more realistic understanding of who they are and what they can do
- are more interested in social activities

Emotional

- compare themselves to others
- are concerned about development and emerging sexually
- see themselves as always on center stage
- are conscious about bodily changes
- are concerned about being liked by friends, social graces, and grooming
- strive for independence, yet want and need parent help
- seek privacy from parents/adults
- want to be a part of something important
- are aware of degrees of emotion and seek to find the right words to describe their feelings
- exaggeration and sarcasm are frequenly used to describe subtle meanings

Eleven-to-thirteen year olds want to be a part of something important.

Intellectual

- need information for making decisions
- find justice and equality to be important issues
- think abstractly and hypothetically
- can solve problems that have more than one variable
- can imagine consequences
- are ready for in-depth, long-term experiences
- have moved from fantasy to realistic focus on their life's goals

---

Activities and Special Considerations

Provide opportunities for:

- engaging in more structured and adult-like activities
- exploring other cultures, foods, languages, and customs
- completing projects (emphasis on precision and perfecting)
- discussing issues and opposite sex with friends
- to making decisions fun, engaging in learning experiences and activities involving the opposite sex, and learning to deal with the opposite sex

---

Fourteen-to-seventeen year olds desire to do things that give an adrenaline rush.

FOURTEEN-TO-SEVENTEEN YEAR OLDS

Physical

- sexual maturity, with accompanying physical and emotional changes
- are concerned about body image; may have complexion problems
- a smaller range in size and maturity exists among peers
- tend to have realistic view of limits to which body can be tested
- desire to do things that give an adrenaline rush, or involve the extraordinary
- boys have enormous appetites; girls tend to watch their weight

Social

- achieving independence from family
- tend to romanticize sexually, but moving toward more realistic understanding
- search for intimacy
- prefer to set own goals rather than accept those set by others
- more accepting of differences
- make and keep commitments
- see adults as fallible
- renegotiate relationships
- want adult leadership roles

Emotional

- have strong identification with admired adult
- desire respect
- beginning to accept and enjoy their own individuality, but still seek status and approval of peer group
- take on multiple roles
- are introspective
- can see self from the viewpoint of others
- can initiate and carry out their own tasks without supervision of others
- desire a role in determining what happens in their world

Intellectual

- beginning of occupational choice
- want their point of view heard

- enjoy demonstrating acquired knowledge
- develop theories to explain how things happen
- tend to lose patience with meaningless activity
- are good problem solvers, but are frustrated when not consulted
- can better understand moral principles
- have an idealistic view of adult life
- beginning to think of leaving home for college, employment, marriage

---

Activities and Special Considerations

Provide opportunities to:

- be a part of the decision-making process
- be empowered to make a difference in what's happening
- show and value their individual differences
- take on responsibility for others
- be a part of coeducational activities
- apply leadership skills
- demonstrate self-expression
- discuss issues and values

Fourteen-to-seventeen year olds tend to have an idealistic view of life.

ADULTS AND SENIOR CITIZENS

Young Adult Characteristics (18-26)

- becoming independent and making it on their own
- focusing on developing marketable skills and knowledge to earn a living
- have a rather idealistic view of adult life
- formulating values and developing a philosophy of life
- beginning to focus on choosing a mate
- interested in expanding base of experiences—travel, vocational experiences, etc.

Adult Characteristics

- achieving satisfaction in their vocation
- assuming social and civic responsibilities
- developing skills that are family-centered
- becoming parents and raising children to become responsible and well-adjusted
- learning to relate to (or care for) parents and older adults
- testing and refining values
- learning to cope with anxiety and frustration
- facing more financial pressures
- encountering increased level of family and work-related stress
- expecting housing that will provide some privacy and comfort

Senior Citizen Characteristics

- adjusting to declining energy and physical changes of aging, ie., decreased flexibility, balance, auditory and visual problems, less strength and endurance, slower reaction time
- building new relationships with grown children and grandchildren
- learning to relate again to their spouse
- coming to terms with their life goals and aspirations
- exhibiting principled, moral reasoning
- may have less financial pressure
- may have a more conservative outlook on life than younger adults
- expecting housing that will provide privacy and accessibility

3

Working with Individual Campers

Children want to be well-liked, to be part of the group, and to seek your approval. It is normal for you to like one camper better than another, as long as you try to treat all campers as fairly as possible. Children imitate the behavior of those who are important to them, without judging whether the behavior is positive or negative. Staff members need to be sure that their individual behavior is worth being mimicked.

Reinforcing Positive Behaviors

As a camp leader, you can encourage good behavior in a number of positive ways, including:

- Establish a caring relationship with campers by opening lines of communication and inviting a camper to come to you if they have a problem. In addition, check in with every camper every day. Ask questions about their day—the best parts and the challenging parts. Build respect and trust by following through on what you say you will do and any promises you make.

- Praise campers to encourage positive behavior. When counselors praise positive acts and ignore the small negative ones, the message is sent that campers must behave in a positive way to gain attention. However, be the adult and intervene when necessary. Don't send a message that you condone actions that put another person down.

- Make sure you tailor your humor so it is understood by children. Children often take seriously something you think of as friendly teasing, funny nicknames, or ribbing.

- Create an atmosphere of cooperation and fun. Use unstructured periods between activities, mornings, and bedtime to create a special time to share feelings, talk, and connect with the group. These moments may provide the best memories of the summer for you and your group.

Good behavior management helps the camper know his or her limits, helps you deliver a quality program, provides time for your attention to each child, helps the camp provide a safe experience, and meets the expectations of parents.

Although campers come from a variety of backgrounds and family experiences, an agreed-upon set of manners can help teach respect for others, gratitude, common courtesies, and basic social skills.

Courtesies of Group Living

Today, many children rarely have a sit-down family dinner where they learn basic table manners or the informal group interactions necessary for group living. Children are often influenced by the media, receive everything they ask for, and have a general lack of respect for authority. Although campers come from a variety of backgrounds and family experiences, an agreed-upon set of manners can help teach respect for others, gratitude, common courtesies, and basic social skills. These courtesies could be expressed as rules—for example, don't litter, be on time, don't interrupt when others are talking, etc. When you discuss conduct based on how everyone should function as a community, the learning is more meaningful than simply a list of rules. Rules may be set by the camp or decided upon by the group. When setting rules of conduct, discuss such questions as:

- What manners are to be observed in the dining area and why are they important? Be sure to include the passing and sharing of food, when the campers can begin eating, when they are dismissed, appropriate table conversation, sitting at the table, and noise levels, along with information on how the food is served and how the tables are prepared and cleaned up.

- What courtesies should everyone show each other?
- How should everyone treat each other's belongings?
- What courtesies should be shown to people who have provided the food, keep the site maintained, provide program or health care, etc.?

Understanding Behavior Clues

If a camper is exhibiting a troublesome behavior, try to understand why the child's behavior is a problem. That individual may have a personality trait, a behavior that irritates you or other campers, or it may be a clue to a bigger problem. This problem may or may not be known by the child. Examples of inappropriate behaviors include practices such as nail biting, poor speech, masturbation, bed-wetting, etc. Such actions may occur initially while the child is at camp and/or be something for which the individual is being treated. Some behaviors may be reactions to you, other campers, or the camp environment.

Keep in mind that campers may demonstrate inappropriate behaviors because they want your attention, desire power, seek revenge, want undue sympathy, or to withdraw socially. The clues that a problem may exist in this regard may be overt actions such as teasing or bullying, using obscene language, showing off, acts of retaliation or rebellion, whining, crying, stubbornness, timidity, or isolation. You may feel annoyed, angry, hurt, sympathetic, burdened, or irritated. Instead of reacting with your feelings, use the clues to try to find out what is bothering the child and work to respond to the problem. It may be helpful to be aware of any notes from parents that may help you deal with the behavior appropriately.

A camper management behavior guide to help you better understand possible prevention and strategies and interventions to deal with individual behaviors and to help you work with your camp on identifying appropriate and consistent consequences is included at the end of this chapter. The following is a list of behaviors or conditions that are either so common or so serious that all counselors should be aware of them and know what to do in case they occur.

Missing Home (Homesickness)

Nearly 95 percent of campers have some feeling of missing home. Such feelings emanate from a distress or impairment, which is caused by an actual or anticipated separation from home. Missing home is characterized by acute longing and preoccupying thoughts of home. Many youngsters miss parents, friends, home, or pets and become despondent and tearful. The term "missing home" is replacing the older term "homesick." As a point of fact in this instance, children are not sick. One of the best preventive measures happens between the camp and the parents to help the children know about the camp environment and the routine and build their confidence before coming to camp. Accordingly, it is your job to continue to raise the campers' comfort levels immediately upon their arrival at camp. While missing home is normal, helping children feel welcome, giving encouraging guidance, and explaining what will happen next can help build their confidence and excitement about being at camp.

Bed-wetting

It is not unusual for younger campers to be faced with the embarrassing situation of bed-wetting in the resident-camp setting. Bed-wetting is not a behavioral problem. No child wants to wake up in a wet bed. Camp is not the place to try to remedy the problem. The role of the counselor is to avoid embarrassment or humiliation of the camper before his or her peers. A procedure for handling the clothes and bedding should be developed so that counselors can deal with the issue quietly and sensitively without any punishment to the camper. Counselors can also help the child by encouraging them to limit their fluid intake after dinner and reminding all campers to go to the bathroom before going to bed. Counselors can also wake the child in the night and walk them to the bathroom.

It also is not unusual for younger campers to "soil" themselves in the process of play or excitement. Again, the key to the situation is to avoid embarrassment or humiliation. The counselor may also help the situation by encouraging a regular time for a bowel movement or reminding the youngster about going to the toilet.

ADD/ADHD

Attention deficit hyperactive disorder is a combination of symptoms that include inattention, destructibility, impulsiveness, and other difficulties associated with attention.

> The percentage of children diagnosed with ADHD has remained fairly constant from 1997 to 2004, and was at 7 percent in 2004. Males were more than two times as likely as females to have been diagnosed with ADHD in 2004—10 percent versus 4 percent respectively. (Child Trends)

Though most children can be overactive at times, a child with ADD/ADHD may act impulsive and inattentive, race ahead, take chances, often interrupt others, and seldom persist in any activity or goal. The camper with ADD/ADHD may also be socially immature and have low self-esteem and high frustration. Such behavior requires considerable supervision. The role of the counselor is to protect the camper from his or her own actions and to try to get the child to participate in normal activities. Some children will be on medication, such as Ritalin®, for this condition; some physicians take the child off their medications for a "vacation" during the summer. In such cases, the healthcare manager and related counselor(s) should be informed. It is also important that as a counselor, you do not "label" a child that is overactive at times as ADD or ADHD, when they have not been diagnosed as such. Always remember that many possible reasons exist for a child's behavior.

Aggression and Violence

Incidents in schools and elsewhere of violence, weapons possession, and threats against others have brought a heightened concern for these types of problems in camp. It is important that staff be trained to recognize warning signs that may precede acts of violence, both in themselves and in others. Although there is no foolproof system for identifying potentially dangerous youngsters, the National School Safety Center identified some behaviors that could indicate a youth's potential for harming him or herself or others, including:

- engaging in tantrums, serious disciplinary problems, and uncontrollable angry outbursts
- name calling, cursing, and abusive language
- making violent threats
- having few or no close friends
- being preoccupied with weapons
- being bullied or bullying peers or younger children
- preferring movies and reading materials dealing with violent themes or rituals
- participating in a gang or an antisocial group on the fringe of peer acceptance
- demonstrating significant mood swings
- threatening suicide

The total percentage of students ages 12 to 18 who reported being targets of hate-related words at school during the previous six months decreased modestly between 1999 and 2003 from 13 percent to 12 percent. A large part of that decrease resulted from a reduction in the percentage of females who were targets of hate-related words—from 14 percent in 1999 to 11 percent in 2003. (Child Trends)

Students were most likely to report hate-related words targeted at a student's race (4 percent in 2003). Two percent of students reported being targeted based on their ethnicity, and between 1 and 2 percent of students reported being targeted for religion, disability, gender or sexual orientation, respectively. (Child Trends)

A growing concern in schools and camps is that of bullying. According to the U.S. Department of Health and Human Services, bullying is defined as an aggressive behavior that is intentional, repeated over time, and involves an imbalance of power or strength. Bullying is a form of victimization and peer abuse. Bullies are often popular, and have power and social status. They usually have strong leadership skills and a small group of friends who encourage their behavior. It is important that staff recognize when these skills are used inappropriately and do not mistake them as positive traits or recognize them with favoritism.

A child who is being bullied may have a hard time defending him or herself. Children who are being bullied may appear moody or depressed, have unexplained bruises or cuts, have torn or missing cloths or belongings, or be reluctant to go some places or participate in some activities. If you suspect a camper is being excluded or bullied, remember that your attention is very powerful and sought by each camper. Your attention will be noticed and show other campers that you believe that he or she is someone worth spending time with. If you feel you should talk with them about it, begin by being supportive, telling the child you are concerned about him or her, and ask questions. Sometimes, youth are reluctant to talk about it. They may be ashamed or believe that an adult cannot or will not do anything about it. It is not helpful to tell them to work it out with the bully or to discuss it in a group with the bully present. However, take care to not build their dependency on you to always rescue them. Help them develop the skills to reduce the emotional reaction they exhibit and feel successful and included in the group. The camper may need help in not blaming themselves and assistance from peers to help them to feel they belong.

As a staff member, you have a critical role to play in helping to stop bullying. It is your responsibility to be aware of the social interactions in the group and to take appropriate action to protect children from serious bullying. Discuss the situation and the consequences for bullying with your supervisor or director. The Camper Behavior Management Chart that is presented later in this chapter offers more information about the prevention and intervention of bullying behavior.

Self-Mutilating Behaviors (SMB)

Experts estimate the incidence of habitual self-injurers is nearly one percent of the total population, with a higher proportion of females than males (National Mental Health Association). The majority of individuals involved in such behavior are between the ages of 12 and 24. Several types of self-abusive and mutilating behaviors exist, including cutting, burning, wound interference, and picking or deliberately harming oneself without suicidal intent. Self-injury works as a coping mechanism to focus on external pain and release tension, relieve stress, and distract those individuals who engage in such behavior from their emotional distress.

Signs and symptoms of self-abusive or mutilating behavior include the presence of fresh, straight, almost surgical, scratches that appear to be done with a razor, needle, or sharp knife, and/or scars from old injuries, small round burns, clusters of small bruises from hitting or pinching. Those individuals who employ such behavior may make excuses for injuries, lock themselves in a bathroom for long periods of time with the water running, and/or have blood or burn stains in the inside of clothing; as well as becoming overly defensive when approached about the possibility of self-abusive behavior.

Teens who cut or mutilate themselves usually feel ashamed and try to hide the signs. SMB is a serious behavior; one you should report any signs or symptoms of to your director as soon as possible.

Suicide

The rate of suicide for persons between the ages of 15 and 24 has nearly tripled since 1960, making it the third leading cause of death in adolescents (National Mental Health Association). Counselors should be alert to signs of depression and the types of symptoms that often precede suicidal behavior. Your camp director probably has procedures for handling such behaviors and knows where to find professional help and resources. Four out of five teens who attempt suicide have given clear warnings. As such, you should pay attention to the following warning signs:

- Suicide threats, direct and indirect
- Obsession with death
- Poems, essays, and drawings that refer to death
- Dramatic change in personality or appearance
- Irrational, bizarre behavior
- Overwhelming sense of guilt, shame, or reflection
- Changed eating or sleeping patterns
- Severe drop in school performance
- Giving away belongings
- Withdraws from friends and family and loses interest in activities
- Acts unusually sad, discouraged, and lonely, and is suddenly calm and happy
- Expresses feelings of hopelessness and/or worthlessness
- Makes statements about not being missed if he or she were gone

- Has family or relationship disruptions, e.g., divorce trauma or ending of a romance

- Demonstrates an unusually long grief reaction from death of a friend, loved one, or even a pet

- Experiences chronic headaches or stomachaches, menstrual irregularities, or apathetic appearance

Any symptomatic behavior for suicide must be considered serious, dealt with carefully, and discussed with the camp director and/or nurse. Make it clear to the camper or staff person that talking about thoughts and feelings is okay, express concern, listen attentively, be empathetic and not judgmental, don't promise confidentiality, stress that suicide is a permanent solution to a temporary problem, and remind them that help is available and that things will get better. Most importantly, don't assume you can help such an individual by yourself. Talk to the director or health-care professional.

Eating Disorders

Anorexia nervosa, bulimia, and binge (BED) are the three eating disorders that are most familiar to the general public. These conditions tend to be more of a problem for girls and are closely associated with depression, low self-esteem, and stress. Adolescent girls who are concerned about weight gain often limit their food intake to a degree that can be problematic, or they may go on eating binges, followed by inducing vomiting to rid themselves of the food. These are not problems that can be solved at camp, unless the camp has a person on staff who has an understanding of and training in treating these maladies. Of all the behavioral difficulties a child might have, this is one that parents are extremely likely to deny, even if confronted with the facts. Because of such parent denial and the somewhat secretive aspect of these disorders, children often arrive at camp without the director being informed of the condition.

On the other hand, all counselors should be aware of what to do if they believe a camper is suffering with an eating disorder. The camper may react with embarrassment or become defensive or angry. Counselors should assure the camper that they will not discuss it with other campers or counselors, but because they really care about the camper and want the camper to be happy, they will report their concern to the director or camp health-care manager. The camper should be able to sense acceptance from the counselor, not shock or disappointment. The counselor should encourage the camper to share feelings at any time he or she is disturbed or upset. (Directors should also be prepared to address a staff member who is suffering from an eating disorder.)

AIDS

Although AIDS is not a behavior, the awareness of persons having the condition can lead to inappropriate behavior patterns or discrimination. Persons with AIDS should be treated as normally as possible. Counselors should be prepared to deal with situations that might cause bleeding or where bleeding might occur. As such, rubber gloves should be available in the camp's living quarters (or in first-aid kits when out of camp), and counselors should be trained in universal precautions. Persons with AIDS ordinarily will understand the dangers that AIDS can have to others. If the issue of AIDS arises in the living group, counselors should be prepared to educate the group to the ways in which AIDS can and cannot be spread to alleviate the fears that some campers may have.

Dealing with Inappropriate Behaviors

Most incidents involving inappropriate behavior and accidents that occur in camp happen when children have free time or are "horsing around." A well-planned program, timed so children are not idle or bored while waiting on others, is key to the prevention of inappropriate behavior. Have songs or games that do not require equipment ready to play while waiting. Be prepared for the wanderer, the camper who always finishes first (or last), changes in the weather, and unexpected delays.

A well-planned program, timed so children are not idle or bored while waiting on others, is key to the prevention of inappropriate behavior.

Discipline is sometimes regarded as an old-fashioned word; it is also a principle that helps channel selfish interests to the welfare of the whole group. Before an inappropriate behavior becomes a discipline issue, consider the following facts that anyone dealing with children should know and understand:

- A child has the occasional need to test the limits.
- A child cannot always manage self-control.
- A child has a strong tendency to support the values of his or her peer group.
- A child has the right to make mistakes.
- A child has a right to be respected as an individual, regardless of any otherwise undesirable features or factors.

Problems can be prevented by helping campers understand their behavior expectations while at camp, earning campers' respect by giving respect, maintaining control, listening, reading signals, and trying to be one step ahead of them at all times.

When discipline is required, there are a few common guidelines to keep in mind. Discipline should always be used sparingly to be effective—if you discipline constantly, it becomes the accepted norm. Discipline should never be used vindictively or emotionally—never let a disciplinary problem put you off balance. The consequences of inappropriate behavior should follow the deed as quickly as possible. Using work as a consequence or a punishment usually creates a poor attitude toward work; the exception might be when the deed created work for others. Physical punishment is never acceptable, nor is verbal abuse, which can be as destructive as physical force. (It should be noted that physical punishment or verbal abuse of a camper by a counselor or another staff member may be symptoms of stress on the part of the individual and grounds for dismissal of the staff member.)

If initial attempts to control or change an unacceptable behavior have failed, the following disciplinary approaches may be helpful:

- Maintain the initiative and try to persuade the camper that it is better to conform.
- Avoid specific threats by using a broad warning of a possible course of action. Rather than saying, "If you do that again, you will be sent home," try "There are consequences for breaking camp rules or for not cooperating." A child may imagine far more fearsome punishments than you can suggest. A specific threat commits you to carry it out or back down and may even dare the child to try you out, whereas a general warning reinforces the idea that compliance will be better than defiance.

- Involve other campers in the process. An indication that peers may not like the behavior brings in a different aspect. For example, in a situation where a group of boys were bullying a younger group, the camp director met separately with the two groups and, by asking questions and gaining specific information, the older boys admitted they had treated the younger boys inappropriately and agreed to face up to their actions. There were no threats or punishment, but the behavior changed.

- Check age characteristics to assess the level of comprehension or the motivation for obeying authority.

- Review the consequences or punishment before setting it. Does it fit the offense? For example, if one camper has peppered another's dessert, is it fair that the culprit goes without his dessert? Is punishment necessary to deter a repetition of the behavior? Any persistently antisocial behavior should not be allowed to pass without some appropriate action. Always keep in mind that some children respond better to negative consequences, while others respond better to rewards or positive reinforcement.

Look for causes of poor behavior. Avoiding difficult situations is a much better approach than having to deal with them once they arise. Campers with too much energy can get into trouble; overtired campers are prone to react badly to provocation. If there is a camper more prone to negative behavior, try to start each day in a manner that will encourage proper behavior. Try to identify campers who might cause problems and have strategies in mind to deal with them if they do occur. Creating a discipline plan can help keep problems from becoming overwhelming.

Consequences should be discussed with all staff and carried out in a consistent manner. Policies should be discussed and decisions made as to when an inappropriate behavior should be discussed with your supervisor and/or the director. The following Camper Behavior Management Guide shows intervention and prevention techniques, as well as a place to note policies and consequences for specific camper behaviors.

Avoiding difficult situations is a much better approach than having to deal with them once they arise.

CAMPER BEHAVIOR MANAGEMENT GUIDE

Behavior	Prevention
Aggression or violence (physical abuse – hitting, shoving, weapons)	Discuss with camper expected and unexpected behavior. Be observant, listen, and try to anticipate problems. Let campers know it's alright to tell the counselor rather than retaliate. Know expectations for intervening if a weapon is involved.
Argumentative or verbally abusive	Discuss rules and expectations for handling conflicts. Discuss the inappropriate behavior such as shouting, cussing, or name calling. Reinforce appropriate behavior such as compromise, cooperation, respect for others, etc.
Boredom/lazy	Discuss with group the schedule for the day or week. Post the schedule where everyone can see what's next. Utilize camper planning or urge camper input on activities they want to do. Be sure the group gets enough sleep at night and rest during the day for their age. Be excited about the program yourself. Design the program with progression.
Bullying	Discuss expectations for behavior and how to gain cooperation from other campers. Make it clear that bullying will not be tolerated at camp. To help children be less dependent on an adult to rescue them in difficult situations, teach them how to lessen the reaction to bullies. Role play and give campers examples of appropriate ways to influence fellow campers. Even though bullies are very skilled at selecting the best time to exercise their peer terror tactics, listen and observe your group to be aware of bullying behaviors that might be happening while you are not there. Male bullies are more likely to employ physical aggression, while girls are more likely to use verbal abuse. If the bully has followers, purposely plan activities to mix the group. Apart from the bully, discuss the impact on the group and explain the consequences of continuing any bullying behavior. Ask other campers in the group for their support and help in including everyone in the group. Do not "label" a child as a bully, because they may enact the role.

Intervention	Consequences & Policy
Move close to the aggressor and immediately intervene. Ask the camper(s) being threatened to move away from the situation. Discuss reasons for this behavior with each aggressor. Help campers deal with whatever prompted this behavior.	If there is a camp policy, what is it? Discuss solutions with camper. Discuss with supervisor. Supervisor discusses with director. Director may decide to call parents or send camper home. Other
Make your requests clear and do not argue or become defensive with the camper. Stop the behavior before it turns into physical abuse. Avoid looking shocked or laughing. Ask each camper to explain the problem. Help campers see alternative ways to solve problems.	If there is a camp policy, what is it? Discuss solutions with camper. Discuss with supervisor. Supervisor discusses with director. Director may decide to call parents or send camper home. Other
Have several games, songs, and ideas of things to do when there are slow times. Try to find a new activity or new twist in doing an activity to challenge them. Recognize their experience and give them some leadership responsibilities. Be sure they understand and perform their responsibilities in the group.	If there is a camp policy. What is it? Discuss solutions with camper. Discuss with supervisor. Supervisor discusses with director. Director may decide to call parents or send camper home. Other
If you observe or suspect bullying, review the rules with the group. Explain why the behavior is inappropriate. Try to build a sense of consciousness about the impact on others, but make the consequences clear. Confront excuses that minimize the behavior or blame others. No matter what provoked the action, bullies are fully responsible for their actions and decisions they made. Talk to the victim in private about his or her feelings and any damage to person or belongings. Encourage them to not react as the bully expects. Since most bullies do not lack self-esteem and often have a sense of entitlement, give the bullying camper opportunities to work with others in a positive way and help them consider alternatives to their unacceptable behavior. If you are able to observe serious bullying behavior, immediately separate the bully from the group and any followers. Stay neutral and calm, but hold the camper accountable for his or her actions and inform the camp administration.	If there is a camp policy, what is it? Discuss solutions with camper. Discuss with supervisor. Supervisor discusses with director. Director may decide to call parents or send camper home. Other

CAMPER BEHAVIOR MANAGEMENT GUIDE

Behavior	Prevention
Constant complaining or whining	Give suggestions on appropriate ways to express your opinion. Utilize camper planning or urge camper input on activities they want to do. Don't let the whining or complaining cause you to lose patience with the child. Encourage the camper to try new things and use positive phrases instead of complaining.
Destructive to property, vandalism	Discuss with campers about respecting the property of the camp and the personal property of others. Know the camp's policy on how to handle and document destructive behavior. Be sure campers know the consequences of destructive behavior. Explain that any valuable property should not have been brought to camp and where it can be kept until the child goes home.
Disrespect for authority (rude, inappropriate with adults)	Model values of respect for authority and gratitude to others in camp. Be understanding but firm when setting limits. Do not change your mind. It is your word, not your reasoning, that matters. Reinforce respectful behavior.
Doesn't follow directions or pay attention	Make directions age-appropriate, clear, and direct. Give directions in small workable steps. With some tasks, you will need to give more individual attention. Ask campers who may have trouble following directions to repeat the directions back to you and make sure they understand them. Reinforce attentive behavior.
Fears (rejection, being out of control being humiliated, failing, etc.)	Campers should be assured on opening day that they are safe. Do not tell scary stories, especially to young children. Empathize with the fear as natural for someone trying something new or being in a new situation. Don't tease or ridicule the child for having the fear. Determine if there is a cause or reason for the fear and discuss the problem with the child.

Intervention	Consequences & Policy
Point out the behavior and explain how it affects others. Try to find out the reasons for complaints and address each with the child. Don't become defensive. Explain to the child that you will not respond to them when they are whining, complaining, or saying I can't do something without trying.	If there is a camp policy, what is it? Discuss solutions with camper. Discuss with supervisor. Supervisor discusses with director. Director may decide to call parents or send camper home. Other
Find out the reason for the destruction (getting even, revenge, seeking attention, fun, power, peer pressure, etc.) and deal with the real problem. Ask campers who destroyed or defaced property to restore it or pay for it. The group behavior chart in Chapter 4 may be helpful if the destruction was by a group of campers.	If there is a camp policy, what is it? Discuss solutions with camper. Discuss with supervisor. Supervisor discusses with director. Director may decide to call parents or send camper home. Other
Even though children may resist and test authority, tell them to stop being rude. Let them know that while they are at camp you are responsible for seeing that rules are followed. Do not back down or tolerate disrespect or lack of cooperation. Turn away from the offending child and when both you and the child are calmer, sit down and spend some time building mutual respect; be firm, but discuss how you might solve the problem together.	If there is a camp policy, what is it? Discuss solutions with camper. Discuss with supervisor. Supervisor discusses with director. Director may decide to call parents or send camper home. Other
Be patient, flexible, and willing to work with campers on a personal basis. When teaching activities, complete one task at a time and ask the camper(s) to demonstrate their understanding. Pair a camper with another camper who can keep focused. Keep eye contact with the child when you are giving instructions.	If there is a camp policy, what is it? Discuss solutions with camper. Discuss with supervisor. Supervisor discusses with director. Director may decide to call parents or send camper home. Other
Make sure other campers do not make fun of the camper's fear. Encourage campers to participate, but do not force the camper to participate in an activity that is uncomfortable. When a camper is afraid to try a new activity or task, break it down into small progressive steps or have him gain confidence by watching others. Pair the frightened camper with a camper who can encourage and support him or her through the experience. Give opportunities for success in activities that the camper enjoys.	If there is a camp policy, what is it? Discuss solutions with camper. Discuss with supervisor. Supervisor discusses with director. Director may decide to call parents or send camper home. Other

CAMPER BEHAVIOR MANAGEMENT GUIDE

Behavior	Prevention
Group instigator	If the camper has followers, purposely plan activities to mix the group. Discuss expectations for behavior and help channel leadership into positive actions. Give campers examples of appropriate ways to influence fellow campers. Help the camper understand the consequences of his or her actions. Consider the reasons for the camper exercising power and influence on others.
Inappropriate language (swearing, use of sexual language)	Explain rules about inappropriate language in camp the first day. Don't shame or put the child down for using language that may be acceptable in their home. Always act as a role model by using appropriate language around children. Give campers examples of accepted language when expressing their disagreements. Compliment campers when you hear them using appropriate language.
Impatience	Give them acceptable ways to voice disagreements. Explain teamwork and ask for ideas of what he or she could do to help others who are slower or less skilled. If the child is impatient at their own skill in doing something, have other options or give them some personal attention with small steps that will lead to success. Have several games, songs, and ideas of things to do when there are slow times or when they have finished before others.
Lying	Emphasize trust and the team or group working together. Don't laugh and inadvertently reward the behavior. Model telling the truth. When you make a mistake, admit it. To promote truthfulness, consistently recognize and praise campers for honesty.

Intervention	Consequences & Policy
Separate the camper from the group and discuss the inappropriate behavior and the negative results of the group's action and their leadership. Help the camper determine alternative positive ways to influence the group. Provide recognition to him or her for positive leadership.	If there is a camp policy, what is it? Discuss solutions with camper. Discuss with supervisor. Supervisor discusses with director. Director may decide to call parents or send camper home. Other
Don't ignore or overreact by showing shock or laughing when a child uses inappropriate language. Speak calmly but firmly about the language that is appropriate at camp. Make sure you let the camper know the behavior is unacceptable in camp so that others don't think it's cool and repeat their actions. Try to find out why the camper is using inappropriate language (anger or out of not knowing better).	If there is a camp policy, what is it? Discuss solutions with camper. Discuss with supervisor. Supervisor discusses with director. Director may decide to call parents or send camper home. Other
Discuss the camper's feelings and help him or her decide what to do when they are feeling impatient (waiting on their turn or waiting for an activity to start or on others in their group.) Recognize and empathize with feelings of frustration and help them deal appropriately with any anger that might come from those feelings. Discuss reasons for needing self-control, being a part of the group, why there are schedules or rules, etc. Encourage the child to complete projects successfully or to help others finish.	If there is a camp policy, what is it? Discuss solutions with camper. Discuss with supervisor. Supervisor discusses with director. Director may decide to call parents or send camper home. Other
Determine the reason(s) for the behavior (attention, belonging, getting respect, etc.) and suggest more appropriate ways to deal with those feelings. Do not "set up a camper to lie" if you know they have done something wrong. Tell them you know what happened and ask for ways to remedy the situation. Talk with the camper about unacceptable behavior and discuss what happens when an individual lies and what happens when they tell the truth. Ignore obvious exaggerations and help the camper tell the difference between reality and wishful thinking.	If there is a camp policy, what is it? Discuss solutions with camper. Discuss with supervisor. Supervisor discusses with director. Director may decide to call parents or send camper home. Other

CAMPER BEHAVIOR MANAGEMENT GUIDE

Behavior	Prevention
Pranks or hazing	Discuss inappropriateness of pranks or hazing-type activities on individuals in your camp. Most end up hurting someone, either emotionally or physically, and could cause a camper to be sent home or be grounds for staff dismissal. Jokes or pranks often grow out of control if left unchecked; if a joke is played on you, accept it and let it die without retaliation. Be sure campers are aware of the consequences of a joke that is hurtful or destructive. Listen and give guidance to conversations that include plans for pranks or retaliation. As a role model, do not instigate pranks or hazing-type activities on other staff or campers.
Put others down (name calling, unkind remarks)	Discuss why it is unacceptable to put others down or call them hurtful names at camp and the consequences of such behavior. Explain that racial or ethnic diversity in the group, as well as different opinions, contribute to the group development and should not be a target for unkind remarks. Talk about how hurtful It may feel if it happened to them. Be a good example when interacting with campers; show them respect. Move around the group and listen to how campers communicate with each other.
Runaway/wanderer	Discuss expectations for where they can and cannot go without a counselor and why. Try to identify why the camper leaves the group. Establish procedures for searching for a missing camper.
Stealing or borrowing without permission	Have campers mark their belongings and be responsible for keeping track of their things. Make expectations clear on the first day about the use of others' belongings and care of their own belongings. Be aware of what each camper is bringing to camp, and if there is something of value, either ask the parents to take it home or ask the director for a safe place to keep it. Know the camp policy regarding searching a campers' or staff members' belongings.

Intervention	Consequences & Policy
Help children to not react in the anticipated manner to a joke played on them. If they ignore or accept it without acknowledgment, the real joke may be on the perpetrators. Jokes or pranks on counselors or on a group that are done carefully and for the campers' benefit could build spirit and model how to be good sports. All adults and staff in camp should behave consistently in handling incidents of pranks, jokes, or hazing-type activities.	If there is a camp policy, what is it? Discuss solutions with camper. Discuss with supervisor. Supervisor discusses with director. Director may decide to call parents or send camper home. Other
Stop the put down or name calling immediately, but don't overreact. Help children to express their feelings about the action that someone does that they do not like, rather than calling them a name. Do not react by laughing or ignoring the behavior, thus giving the camper the sense you are condoning such behavior. Correct the camper in a calm voice and manner. The camper may not realize that what he or she said is not appropriate or hurtful.	If there is a camp policy, what is it? Discuss solutions with camper. Discuss with supervisor. Supervisor discusses with director. Director may decide to call parents or send camper home. Other
If the child is missing, stay calm, and keep the rest of the group calm and together. Check obvious places, ask others about when last seen, frame of mind, clothing, etc., and report, as per procedures for a search. If the child is constantly wandering away from the group, remind them of the rules, safety reasons for staying with the group, and consequences for continuing the behavior. Discuss the problem with the whole group and ask for their help in keeping everyone together (establishing a buddy system, number off participants, and periodically ask for a call-off, etc.)	If there is a camp policy, what is it? Discuss solutions with camper. Discuss with supervisor. Supervisor discusses with director. Director may decide to call parents or send camper home. Other
If there has been an accusation, be sensitive to both parties' feelings, and try to determine if the action was stealing, a mistake, or used with or without permission. If you know who is stealing, the stolen item should be returned with an apology, and the incident discussed with the director. If you're unsure who is stealing, have a group meeting and determine how the missing item should be returned.	If there is a camp policy, what is it? Discuss solutions with camper. Discuss with supervisor. Supervisor discusses with director. Director may decide to call parents or send camper home. Other

CAMPER BEHAVIOR MANAGEMENT GUIDE

Behavior	Prevention
Substance abuse (smoking, alcohol, drugs)	Policies should be in the material sent to campers and parents before camp starts. Be a positive role model and follow the camp policies yourself. Do not discuss with campers whether you smoke, drink, or have ever tried drugs. Make campers aware of the camp's policies, the laws in their state, and the consequences of a camper caught with drugs, alcohol, or tobacco. Know the camp policy regarding searching a camper's or staff member's belongings.
Showing-off or clowning	Do not laugh or encourage show-off behavior; explain that there may be a more appropriate time to tell the story or act in that manner. Help the campers understand expectations for accomplishing a task or activity and the time period available. Explain the importance of being serious, listening, and paying attention to instructions either so that they can participate in activities or for safety reasons.
Tattling, gossip, blaming others	Discuss why it is unacceptable to gossip about others and the consequences of such behavior. Talk about how hurtful it may feel if it happened to them. Do team-building activities. Try to determine the reason for tattling on others (to win favor or to get others in trouble). Don't label the child as tattletale or gossip. Be a good example when interacting with campers; show them respect. Move around the group and listen to how campers communicate with each other.

Intervention	Consequences & Policy
Explain that they have broken a camp policy and follow procedures about consequences. Be sure that you do not reach premature conclusions and be sure to follow procedures about searching belongings and confiscating materials.	If there is a camp policy, what is it? Discuss solutions with camper. Discuss with supervisor. Supervisor discusses with director. Director may decide to call parents or send camper home. Other
Take the camper aside and explain why his or her behavior is interruptive and not appropriate. Try to access the reasons for the behavior and ask for a serious answer. Try to channel the action into a positive role in a skit or other appropriate activity. Once the camper's behavior is given attention (positive or negative) by other members of the group, the behavior may be difficult for the child to control, and it may be encouraged by the other campers. A discussion with the entire group about the interruptive behavior may be necessary for the group to continue in a positive manner.	If there is a camp policy, what is it? Discuss solutions with camper. Discuss with supervisor. Supervisor discusses with director. Director may decide to call parents or send camper home. Other
Help the camper to express their feelings appropriately about the action that someone does that they do not like. Listen to both sides of a situation and discuss more appropriate ways to handle the situation. Explain that you know they may be trying to help you, but correcting others' behavior is your job. Do not ignore the behavior, thus giving camper the sense you are condoning such behavior. Reward other ways to gain attention, without hurting others. The camper may not realize that what he or she said is not appropriate or hurtful, or they may be struggling with the rules themselves and want their good behavior to be noticed.	If there is a camp policy, what is it? Discuss solutions with camper. Discuss with supervisor. Supervisor discusses with director. Director may decide to call parents or send camper home. Other

CAMPER BEHAVIOR MANAGEMENT GUIDE

Behavior	Prevention
Testing rules, limits	Make sure your rules and expectations are reasonable and coincide with camp expectations. Have the group identify their own rules for functioning safely as a group at camp. Review these rules on the first day; explain why each rule is important. Remember to be consistent in enforcing the rules and in praising campers who follow the rules.
Unusual sexual behavior (inappropriate touching of others or themselves, exposure, etc.)	Discuss privacy issues, personal space, and unwanted touching of other campers. Unusual sexual behavior may be an indication of sexual abuse in the home or other settings or an indication the child has been stimulated by magazines, TV, or observation of an older sister or brother. Discuss such behaviors with the director.
Victim/revenge	Discuss what to do if you are being bullied. Victims are often physically weak or emotionally vulnerable and will not seek help. Recognize that this cycle is very difficult to stop and that children can be very cruel to each other. Do teambuilding and bonding activities that put a rejected child on equal footing with others. Try to match children in the group, so that they are at the same maturity level. There may be a struggle between the victim (helpless individual who needs protection) and the popular leader for the attention of the counselor.

Intervention	Consequences & Policy
Talk to the camper away from the group about his or her behavior. Review the rules with the whole group and ask for their help in reinforcing positive behavior. Give campers the opportunity to challenge rules appropriately. Meet with other staff and the director to discuss productive ways to challenge authority and how to prevent difficulties.	If there is a camp policy, what is it? Discuss solutions with camper. Discuss with supervisor. Supervisor discusses with director. Director may decide to call parents or send camper home. Other
If you observe inappropriate touching of a camper by another camper, speak directly to the camper about the action. Do not assume campers know the difference between appropriate and inappropriate touching. Follow the camp's procedures for reporting and documentation of such incidents.	If there is a camp policy, what is it? Discuss solutions with camper. Discuss with supervisor. Supervisor discusses with director. Director may decide to call parents or send camper home. Other
Deal with the aggressors, but realize that reprimanding the whole group may make it worse for the scapegoat. Teach the child who is being teased new ways to respond. Being angry or crying will just encourage additional attacks. Acknowledge how difficult it is to ignore teasing, make suggestions, and practice answers with him or her. The group may suggest that the scapegoat be placed in another group or stay with the counselor, which if allowed, may just perpetuate their rejection of the child. Listen and be aware of children being victimized and of any retaliation or revenge planned by the victim(s).	If there is a camp policy, what is it? Discuss solutions with camper. Discuss with supervisor. Supervisor discusses with director. Director may decide to call parents or send camper home. Other

4

Working with Groups

The uniqueness of the camp experience is more than a series of activities to engage children; it is a group-living experience. Individuals are not only brought together to share common experiences in an outdoor setting, but they are encouraged to develop a cohesive group with positive interpersonal relationships and social skills. They must develop mutual respect and trust that is greater than roles based upon one's sex, race, economic situation, or physical condition.

To successfully work with camper groups, it is important that staff agree on the appropriate and inappropriate behavior of campers, the consistent behavior management and supervisory techniques that will be employed, and the policies or consequences of inappropriate behaviors in camp. Insurance records and analysis of accidents and behavior incidents in camp are very closely tied to supervision issues, issues of what "on duty" means, free or unscheduled time, etc. The camp that enumerates a lengthy list of rules immediately upon arrival at camp invites campers to "test the limits" or violate rules. Yet, some rules are necessary in any community. The staff's method of applying those rules consistently and educating youth about the reasons for the rules and gaining their participation in setting and agreeing to them is critical.

What about being a friend? From a risk-management viewpoint, as well as a control and organizational viewpoint, counselors must maintain their positions as leaders. Too often, leaders aspire to be the group's best friend and lose sight of their official role, which causes them to face decisions that compromise their responsibility and authority. Being an effective leader is a delicate weave of traits and skills, including integrity, self-confidence, empathy, and the ability to foster positive group development and individual growth. The elimination of any single trait or characteristic weakens the fabric and the overall effectiveness of the leader.

The first part of this book identified strategies for prevention and intervention in supervising and dealing with an individual's behavior. This chapter provides strategies for dealing with different types of group behaviors.

Setting the Tone for Group Development

In any group activity, a purpose, goal, or specific task should be identified and completed. Individuals with different talents and strengths become a group as they learn about and from each other and accept a common goal. This acceptance and common pursuit of a goal, if orchestrated properly, will supersede individual differences. As you begin working with any group, be sure the group is comfortable with each other. Start with get-acquainted activities and then progress to more personal sharing. In this regard, among the steps that you can take are the following:

- Get and hold the group's attention.
- Stand or sit where everyone can see you.
- Speak just loudly enough for everyone to hear you.
- Ask the group for ideas about how they should treat each other (i.e., no put-downs), listen to each other, help each other, etc.
- Participate with the group in the activities whenever possible.
- Listen and encourage each camper to participate and share.
- Try to make everything, even mistakes, into a learning experience.

Individuals with different talents and strengths become a group as they learn about and from each other and accept a common goal.

Cycles of Group Activity Planning

Throughout the day, the session, and program activities, certain cycles occur that should be considered in planning:

- Daily cycle—Each day should be planned so that the activities are in cycles that match the campers' energy level and end with settling down campers for the evening. For example, begin the day with a high-energy activity, such as swimming, games, ropes course, etc. Then, move the campers into a more quiet and restful period with crafts, stories, thought-provoking activities, or discussions, etc. After this calming period, add more high-energy activity, and end the day with quiet activities.
- Session cycle—Despite the length of a camp session, it should always begin with activities that raise the comfort level within the camper group and end with returning home. (See the stages of group development chart.)
- Program activity cycle—Be sure to include an introduction to each activity where the activity is explained, safety rules are discussed, and equipment gathered. Once the activity is completed, allow time to clean up and to debrief the campers on the skills or concepts learned during the program. (See the section on debriefing an activity.)

Group Building

Productive group behavior is dependent on both the group's attitude and the counselor's attitude and actions. Any group should include the following attributes: guidance, organization, coordination, delegation of authority, dependability, fairness, consideration, respect, and consistency. When these qualities are present in a counselor, the morale and efficiency of the group will be higher.

As a counselor, you play a critical role in every stage of group development. The stages of group development chart details the various stages of group development, possible group reactions, and your specific role at each stage.

Camper Planning

Camper or group planning, as a teaching method, helps the group establish a working relationship and helps produce a systematic approach to providing order, clarity, and purpose to their task. For example, campers who help set their own rules are more likely to follow them and help hold their group accountable for the agreed-upon rules for their group.

Learning as a Part of the Group Process

Learning is more interesting and fun for campers if a variety of methods are used. The method chosen should be appropriate for the participants' age. Some methods fit better with the subject matter being taught. For example, a discussion would not be as effective as a demonstration for tying knots. Some skills can best be learned with two or more methods, for example, brainstorming ideas for safety rules, and then discussing the ideas and deciding which are appropriate for the group.

Discussion, demonstration and practice (by the counselor or a group member), observation, idea generation, sharing, and debriefing an activity are all effective methods to use with a group. Any one method will not work for all situations or for all learners.

❑ Discussion. Spontaneous discussion and involvement will not occur naturally if group members feel inhibited. Participation in the group discussion requires involvement, motivation to contribute, and acceptance of responsibility for one's actions. The following steps can help encourage participation in discussions:

- Praise and thank those contributing.
- Mediate differences of opinion.
- Provide the information they need for the discussion.
- Have several ideas to help them get started or to regenerate enthusiasm.
- Refocus the group's attention when necessary.
- Summarize the discussion.

Discussion, demonstration and practice (by the counselor or a group member), observation, idea generation, sharing, and debriefing an activity are all effective methods to use with a group.

STAGES OF GROUP DEVELOPMENT

Stage	Group Indicators	Counselor's Role
1. Saying hello	Feeling insecure and unsure of themselves. Being concerned about how they fit into group. Showing excitement about camp, but having some separation anxieties.	Clarify expectations. Build comfort with camp. Avoid discussing personal feelings or close physical contact. Encourage interaction, trust, and involvement. Use name games and icebreakers to keep the group active.
2. Saying who	Sorting it out. Picking friends. Developing roles in the group. Developing norms and common ground. Getting to know how the counselor works.	Watch for power struggles and cliques. Encourage openness and sharing. Help with conflict resolution. Organize different subgroup structures for activities. Use cooperation games.
3. Saying why	Understanding their role. Building the team. Depending on each other. Beginning to work and share space together. Challenging leadership.	Help the group assume responsibility for actions and decisions. Help with group decisions and problem-solving. Use team-building games and group projects.
4. Saying we	Acknowledging individual strengths in each other. Developing respect for each other. Becoming interdependent. Finding success in their contribution. Sharing feelings.	Allow time for creativity and discussion. Encourage group challenge and adventure. Watch for exhaustion. Acknowledge individual and group accomplishments.
5. Saying good-bye	Having mixed feelings about leaving and going home. Recognizing growth and change. Wanting to maintain ties with camp and others in the group.	Encourage reflection. Reward accomplishments. Help transfer what they learned to home and school environment. Help with re-entry.

❑ Demonstration and practice. Children learn by doing. To keep the campers' interest when you are teaching a skill, you need to be able to demonstrate the skill and have them practice it. It is hard to patiently and slowly demonstrate each step of a skill you know well and do easily. Try your demonstration first with another counselor. Be sure to:

- Break down the demonstration into easy steps.
- Have the group practice each step and encourage their successful progress.
- Make the presentation fun and nonthreatening.
- Include enough materials for each participant to be involved.
- Repeat and review.

❏ Observation. Many observation games or activities exist that can be used to increase campers' interest or curiosity. These teaching methods sharpen campers' skills, create excitement, and make learning fun. Use the following ideas to help your campers learn to be more observant:

- Build on campers' observations and encourage comments.
- Encourage campers to use all their senses.
- Model observation by relating stories to things observed.
- Don't rush everywhere; take time to look around you.
- Observe from a different point of view, e. g., taking a frog's-eye view, walking backwards, or asking questions that will stimulate interest.
- Don't worry if you don't have the answers; you can find them out together with your campers.

❏ Generating and sharing ideas. In the early stages of group development, members may be shy or reluctant to share their opinions about program, rules, ways to solve a problem, planning activities, etc. To motivate campers to participate and get involved in the camper group, use the following steps:

- Define the purpose of gathering ideas and the allotted time limits for the process.
- Set up a safe environment for generating ideas.
- Tell campers there are no bad ideas.
- Appoint someone to write the ideas down.
- Discuss and prioritize the best ideas.
- If the campers are older, instruct the campers to pair off or gather in small groups to develop suggestions that can be reported to the whole group.

❏ Debriefing an activity. After completing an activity, ask the group members about the experience. A game or activity may increase interest or curiosity and lead to other activities or discussions about how the group members worked together. Debriefing can be more formalized, taking some time to discuss what happened, how it made them feel, and then, what they learned and how they can use the information when they go home. It can also be a discussion while moving to the next activity or toward the end of the day. Often, campers just think about doing new things and having fun together and not the other benefits. A good leader can be more intentional about the outcome and encourage campers to think about the activity and share their feelings. The following suggestions can enhance the debriefing effort:

- Build on and encourage comments.
- Use all of the senses. What did campers see, hear, feel, etc.?
- Take time to listen to campers and remind them to listen to each other.
- Invite everyone to participate.
- Ask key questions that will stimulate interest.
- Beware that it is okay not to have all the answers—learn together.
- Ask how campers will use what they learned at home.

Ideas for including everyone in a discussion (or taking turns):

- Take a long rope, pass it around the circle, and ask each person to add a thought to the discussion by tying a knot in the rope.
- Find a special looking stick and call it a "talking stick" (it might be one you want to decorate and save for later discussions). Explain that only the person with the stick can talk.
- Form a circle and ask the participants to think of one word that describes the activity. Go around the circle and share the word. Then, ask for two words that describe how they feel…then three words that describe what they learned.
- Before the activity (or the day), explain that you are going to say "cheese!" and they are to take a mental picture of the situation they are in. After the activity, ask each person to describe one "picture" they remember.

Inappropriate Group Behavior

When dealing with a large number of youth from a variety of backgrounds and family patterns, in a setting where they can try new and different behaviors, there will often be instances when those behaviors will be unacceptable and require discipline. When a group is acting inappropriately, it is important to identify what is happening in the group. What stage of group development are they in? Are there power struggles and cliques? Are they functioning as a strong group, but finding more joy in working together on disruptive and inappropriate activities, because they are either bored with the program or the way they are being treated?

Sometimes change in the program or staff initiates a negative team response in the campers. What are their discussions and concerns about? Are there a few strong leaders in the group who are instigating the group behavior? The following are some of the key issues involved in group behavior—each of which also includes a list of suggestions for dealing with inappropriate group behavior.

Peer Pressure

Campers often need help distinguishing between needing to be part of the group and negative peer pressure. As children get older, the opinions and acceptance of their peers become more and more important. As part of a group, children may ask themselves if participation will get them into trouble, harm themselves or someone else, or if they want to participate just because they don't want to be left out. The counselor can praise those campers who are willing to voice their opinions and help campers deal with peer pressure by discussing situations where it is difficult to stand against the group and why it is important to tell others how you feel.

Stereotypes/Prejudices

Children are influenced by the role models observed on television, their parents and teachers, and the expectations they are comfortable with from their own culture. Camps serve different camper populations. Some are all the same sex, while others target a specific economic level, religious group, or racial or ethnic group. These can be barriers to group development. People tend to act out behaviors that reinforce stereotypes or reflect their own experiences. The example you set reflects your own values, expectations, background, and experiences. This factor is of great importance because children tend to imitate their adult role models. Your challenge, as a counselor, is to examine your own prejudices, feelings, and actions and determine the expectations the camp has for you as a role model for its campers.

Whether you are working with a group of girls, a group of boys, or a coed group, you should be aware of several key characteristics within your camper group. In resolving conflicts, girls tend to be more verbal, and boys more physical. Girls are more worried about how others feel and take criticism personally. Boys are more likely to deny feelings of vulnerability and label each other as strong or weak. Counselors need to distinguish between the stereotypical feelings of girls or boys and real conflict.

Group Rowdiness

The group can get carried away, especially in the second and third stage of group development when the group is struggling for roles and testing authority. Some competitive activities over-stimulate the group and lead to inappropriate group behaviors against another group. Also, negative leadership may emerge from the group during times when the group is bored or waiting, being transported, or otherwise not in structured activities. The counselor should be sensitive to what is happening in the group, and identify warning signs and ways to gain control.

Practical Jokes

Pranks and hazing are discussed in the camper behavior chart that appeared in Chapter 3. Practical jokes can often become inappropriate group behavior as the stages of the group progresses. The joke can become something against another group, a staff member, or an individual, or it can involve behavior that is destructive of personal or camp property. Many pranks begin as team- or group-building fun and develop into a series of retaliation and destructive behaviors. The counselor needs to be aware of the ramifications and appropriateness of the group's behavior.

Practical jokes can often become inappropriate group behavior as the stages of the group progresses.

Camper-to-Camper Abuse

Camper-to-camper abuse has been a growing concern at camp, and what in the past may have been considered a prank or hazing is today considered abuse. Some of the sexual behavior identified as a normal aspect of human growth and development may become abuse when a camper exhibits that behavior with a younger camper or by force on a peer. Occasionally, there are children who are unable to judge the appropriateness of sexual or physical abusive behavior because of their family or personal experiences.

Bullies may gain the power they seek by trying to gather support from other members of the group. In addition to physical or sexual abuse, this bullying behavior can involve emotional abuse that includes teasing, name calling, gossiping, exclusionary actions, threats, or embarrassment in front of others. Such abuse can begin on the internet between returning campers or staff before camp and continue to develop as the group evolves.

A significant amount of bullying behavior is also often observed among the staff. Establishing boundaries with staff and campers around bullying behavior is no different than addressing other inappropriate behaviors. As role models, an agreed-upon, no-tolerance plan will help you demonstrate the appropriate behavior you expect to see at all levels. If you have any questions about a camper's or another staff member's behavior, it is wise to discuss the matter with your camp director.

Ideas for Dealing With Inappropriate Group Behaviors

The following suggestions can help you deal with inappropriate group behaviors:

- Explain the reason for camp rules, and ask the group to establish some group rules.
- Listen to what the campers are saying, not just how they are acting.
- Don't be judgmental, and look for the cause of the behavior.
- Support the campers as they try to find a solution.
- Model the behavior you want to see in your campers.
- Deliberately mix campers into different subgroups.
- Talk with campers in a nonshaming, nonaccusatory way.
- Explain that it is normal to have different opinions and the importance of respecting the opinion of others.
- Help campers discuss their feelings of anger, resentment, not belonging, power, fear, shame, etc. Provide opportunities for campers to discuss these feelings in private.
- Discuss what it means to be a friend and what it means to be a part of the group.
- Play cooperative and team-building games.
- Talk to other counselors and administrative staff about the problems you are having with your group or with other staff.

5

How to Measure Your Success

This book, along with your training and experience, is designed to help prepare you to be able to reinforce positive or appropriate behaviors and deal with the inappropriate ones. Don't wait until the end of camp to look at how successful you are with your campers. Whenever feasible, take an occasional look at your attitude and actions that might contribute to your success. Does your attitude need adjusting? Now that you have some experience in working with campers and other staff, the following points may help you examine your feelings and, in the process, become more effective:

- Attitude is contagious—Be optimistic and make it your goal to help campers begin each day with a positive attitude.

- Share your expectations—Help campers understand the expectations for their behavior while they're at camp and reinforce positive behaviors.

- Problems have a way of growing—Set goals to prevent problems, and then promptly deal with inappropriate behaviors.

- Earn the respect of your campers by giving respect—Treat the behavior of campers consistently, be fair, maintain control, listen and read signals, and try to be one step ahead of them.

- Share your struggles—Look for ways to work with other staff on a solution to behavior problems you may be having with your campers and share your successes.

Evaluating Your Success as a Counselor

Periodically do a self-assessment to rate how you are handling stress and dealing with your campers. Use the following scale to rate how you were feeling: 1 = always, 2 = most of the time, 3 = sometimes, 4 = rarely.

SELF-ASSESSMENT QUERIES

___ Did I have an overall feeling of success at meeting the camp's goals and outcomes for campers?

___ Did I personally interact and participate with campers?

___ Did I handle behavior problems promptly, fairly, and consistently?

___ Can I control my temper and keep from getting impatient with campers and other staff?

___ Am I able to keep my tone of voice from being too harsh or commanding?

___ Was I able to talk and listen to each camper?

___ Was I able to enforce rules and policies of the camp?

___ Did I show enthusiasm and was my attitude positive and encouraging?

___ Did I treat the campers with respect?

___ Am I helping campers to grow intellectually and socially?

___ Was I a good role model?

___ Did I show honest support of the other staff?

___ Did I help where needed, even if it was not my responsibility?

___ Did I maintain a good sense of humor?

___ Did I get enough sleep?

___ Did I eat well?

___ Did I make time for myself?

___ Do I recognize my limits?

___ Is there someone I can confide in?

Your supervisor may have several conferences with you during the summer to help you be more successful at camp. Your self-assessment or your supervisor's evaluation may give you ideas on handling some behavior problems you have been having with your campers or other staff. You may even identify some ideas for in-service training that may help all counselors.

The camp may also have a camper and/or parent evaluation process or form to find out what the campers and their parents felt about the camp experience and how successful the camp was at achieving the camp's goals and outcomes. If these are discussed at a staff meeting before the end of camp, this type of evaluation may give counselors some ideas to use with new campers.

Your experience this summer as a counselor or staff member at camp will help you understand how you work with others and will be an excellent indicator of the future directions you may want to take in your life.

Index

About the ACA

The American Camp Association (ACA) is a community of camp professionals dedicated to ensuring the high quality of camp programs, a greater public understanding of and support for the value of the camp experience, and an increase in the number of children, youth, and adults of all social, cultural, and economic groups who participate in the camp experience. Established in 1910, ACA operates as a private, nonprofit educational organization with members in all 50 states and several foreign countries. Its members represent a diverse constituency of camp owners and directors, executives, educators, clergy, businesses, consultants, camp and organization staff members, volunteers, students, retirees, and other individuals associated with the operation of camps for children and adults.

The services provided by ACA include educational programs and conferences, accreditation services, networking, monitoring of legislation at the federal and state levels, *Camping Magazine*, public relations efforts, and an on-line bookstore providing educational resources related to camping, conferencing, and outdoor education. ACA also serves as a consultant and advisor to many state and federal agencies in the field of camping and to colleges and universities in the fields of outdoor education and recreation.

The programs of the Association are administered through numerous local sections. Members belong to the national organization and to a local section responsible for delivering services, including the accreditation programs. Section and national officers are elected by the membership and serve without pay. The organization is supported primarily by the dues and contributions of its members. Other support comes from conference fees, the sale of publications, project grants, and fees for services.

The ACA community of camps promote active participation, caring relationships, and focus on the emotional, social, spiritual, and physical growth of an individual. Camps vary in their purpose and desired outcomes, but each encourages risk taking, valuing the resources of the natural world, healthy lifestyles, and learning through a variety of fun and life-changing experiences.

Because of our diverse membership and exceptional programs, children and adults have the opportunity to learn powerful lessons in community, characterbuilding, skill development, and healthy living. As a leading authority in child development, the ACA works to preserve, promote, and improve the camp experience.

About the Author

Connie Coutellier is a trainer, consultant, and author. She is a national field executive for Camp Fire USA and was the national president and director of professional development for the American Camp Association. A list of the books she has written includes *Day Camp From Day One, The Management of Risks and Emergencies,* and *The Outdoor Book*. She has over 15 years of experience as a camp director and over 25 years of experience in youth development and outdoor program administration training and development. She has written online training courses, assisted in the writing of the *ACA Outdoor Living Skills* books, and served as a consultant for both the development of the *Basic Camp Management* book and the curriculum for the ACA camp director courses.